Poetry and Other Musings

VOLUME ONE

MICHAEL CRAIN

Poetry and Other Musings
Copyright © 2024 by Michael Crain

All rights reserved. No part of this publication may be reproduced, distributed, or transmitted in any form or by any means, including photocopying, recording, or other electronic or mechanical methods, without the prior written permission of the author, except in the case of brief quotations embodied in critical reviews and certain other non-commercial uses permitted by copyright law.

Tellwell Talent
www.tellwell.ca

ISBN
978-1-77962-340-9 (Paperback)

Dedications

For Mum and Dad, thank you for your love
and support even beyond this mortal coil.

For Geoff, thank you for our friendship
and your kindness all these years.

For the Van. U. Poetry Group, thank you for giving
me a creative outlet that I so desperately need.

Dr. Hill,
 Thanks so much for the excellent job you do in looking after my dental health. I hope you enjoy the book!

~ Michael

Hey Tay,

Love to know about your thoughts re: this!

Love
DAD

Table of Contents

The Bearded Tree 1
Amma's Roses 2
Urban Street 3
Dreamscape 4
Spring 5
Waiting 6
Your Soft, Sweet Self 7
The First Garden 8
Loss 9
Before the Show 10
The Looking Glass 11
The Tiger in the Cave 12
Some Treasurers Along the Way 13
Beautiful Moon 14
The Bitch About the Beach 15
Not Being Remembered 16
Six Feet Apart 17
The New Blue 18
A Different Path 19
Gone 20
A New Cat 21
Without Our Consent 22
The Wild One 23
The Cat Poem 24

Schemes	25
What Follows	26
Summertime	27
Missing Out on Home	28
Beyond the Trees	29
Devouring Wood	30
The Leaf	31
The Inevitable	32
Monsters	33
The Grave	34
Waking to the Wild One	35
Perpetual Darkness	36
Out of Reach	37
New Land	38
The Good	39
Admire the Mystery	40
The Day the Sirens Came	41
For Geoff	48
I Left My Brain in My Other Coat Pocket	49
Little Bird	50
Precipice	51
The Vale	52
The Mouse	53
Birthdays	54
Back to Bed	55
The Snow	56
Dark Days	57
The Cork	58
Afraid	59
Crow	60
Dreams	61
Chopsticks	62

The Bearded Tree

To sit and watch and smoke and read,
Once upon a bearded sleave,
I saw her and then did grieve.
My life is death personified,
It cuts me deep just like a knife,
And then I weep and cry for life.
And then I die and am reborn.
Like the sun unto the mourn,
There is no life but sandy shoren.
And then my death comes unto me,
It sweeps me like a bearded tree,
And I am left with Trinity, the three.

Amma's Roses

No one grew roses like you: all different kinds, all different colours. You were proud of your beautiful garden, but you were always most proud of your roses. Yellow, orange, pink, and red are the ones I remember. I used to love walking up your path and seeing the roses there. They smelled so sweet and lovely, just like you were.

They stayed outside the house until the day you were gone. When you were gone, outside family came and stole them from the yard. I used to remember you tending them and loving them, but now there is an empty space left where they were, just like the space left when you went. I miss how you loved them and looked after them. Most of all I miss you and how we loved each other.

Urban Street

Nowhere does the mountain of the rich and the valley of the poor meet more than on an urban street. Commercialism, both crass and sometimes necessary, rears its head here. The poor want money. The coffee shop wants money. The bus and taxi want money. The corner stores, the clothing stores, the bookstore, the fast-food outlet, the cinema all want money. Travelling through an urban street makes you feel like you serve only one purpose, like you're made for one thing only. No wonder zombies became so popular. We're meant to consume just like them.

All I want is to pass through, to get where I am going and not lose my soul or my money. No food from the food cart, no new shoes, no tickets to the upcoming show, just get me home where I can consume my dinner in peace and let the urban street consume someone else. No thanks, no thank you, no. I'll keep moving and you keep your teeth to yourself. I'd only give you indigestion anyhow.

Dreamscape

Each night, but not every night, my mind goes someplace else. Sometimes happy, sometimes anxious, the surreal land of sleep becomes the real land of memories and things not yet accomplished. The stuff of dreams is the unreal, the not created, the yet to be born, and things whose time has come and gone.

Each night that I am visited by a dream, I could be chased through fields of grass or sewers of sludge or up and down flights of stairs in old homes. No place can hide me, and so I run endlessly from an unknown pursuer known to me as anxiety.

Some dreams are sweet, of past family and friends who I will not see again in waking hours. How I wish I could see them again in waking hours. How I wish dreams could be more tangible than they are.

Spring

Spring is duality. New life comes through incredible energy, seeking to find its way into a new world. It takes life to build life, as often the old falls away from the new. I have lost so much to spring, taking the old to build the new.

The energy that it takes for new life can be such a drain, like a ball and chain pulling you under the current, down and down to drown at this energy source. Spring could not be built without the choking out of the old. I have watched spring take a lot of life to create the new.

I fear spring. I fear spring and what it might take next. I fear spring and the life it claims each time it comes. The duality frightens me, and I am left only with the hope that summer will come quickly.

Waiting

We wait for so many things: time to pass, our order to arrive, life to happen. I've heard of an aptly named show called *Waiting for God*. This is an interesting way of saying waiting for the end. But which is it that we are waiting for? Are we waiting for life or are we waiting for death? Is it possible that it's both? We are waiting for life to continue and each note to change in the song, however well played it might be. We are also waiting for the end. I hope these two blend nicely when the time comes, when the waiting is over.

Your Soft, Sweet Self

Your fur smelled divine to me as I held you close to my face. I always loved the way you smelled. Christmas morning was your day to love the world, with all the presents being opened with wrapping paper everywhere. You loved exploring and playing in the aftermath of presents being opened. You always got your own toy that day which you would play with and love.

Oh, my sweet girl, how I miss you and your soft sweet smell. Now I remember you each day as I see the world how you saw it.

The First Garden

The first thing ever was a garden. I wonder what it looked like full of plants and animals, speaking animals at that, and fruit containing knowledge. I wonder what paths weaved through the garden, and which path the serpent took to find the people there.

I wonder how luscious that fruit must have looked and seemed in that idyllic setting. How would it have smelled and felt to the touch? How would it have been with teeth ripping into it and tasting the sweet juice and flesh on the tongue? I wonder if we will ever see a garden quite like that one again. I wonder if the serpent wonders the same thing.

Loss

How much more is there to lose? I feel like life is a measuring stick of loss, with inches of age and miles of growing older. Age takes a little more from you with each passing year. Your sight goes, your hearing goes, your knees go. Bit by bit you deteriorate with age. Are we grinding ourselves down into dust? Ashes to ashes and all the rest?

As things fade, let's hope there is gain as well. Seasons pass and so will we, fading to a large degree, an ending to the entity of me.

Before the Show

The darkness of the movie theatre leads to the anticipation of the show to come. Across the sticky floor you find what seem like good seats with a decent view. You hope that no one with big hair comes and sits in front of you.

The smell of stale popcorn and fermenting soft drinks hangs in the air, turning your stomach from ever wanting anything from the candy counter. The lights soon fade down, leaving the theatre as dim as dusk while the curtain slowly parts or rises, changing the consciousness of the room. Sometimes good, sometimes bad, sometimes too long, the previews eventually end. The show begins and all else drops and fades away.

The Looking Glass

Looking through the Looking Glass,
At a long ago past,
Moving to the future now,
The Looking Glass then takes a bow.
Of all the times I've tried to be
Past, present, and the future me,
The one thing I have always known:
The Looking Glass is magic blown.
If I can spy a future me
Through the Looking Glass I see
I wonder if I'd see thee
Or someone else reflected back at me.
I wonder if I'd recognize
The person there who's in disguise
Or realize that it's the same old me,
The person that I'll always be.

The Tiger in the Cave

Hello, Tiger in the cave. My, what big paws you have. Please don't eat me! I know you think that I might be a sweet treat, but really I'm not that tasty. I wonder how long you have been in this cave with your big paws and your strong breath. Have you ever thought of leaving, or are you stuck here somehow?

The bones around your cave indicate that you have not had to go far to find a meal. Do you miss hunting, or are you pleased being in your cave all day? Oh, please don't eat me, kind Tiger. I would only give you a tummy ache!

Some Treasurers Along the Way

Searching for the right words to express feeling can be elusive, like an idea lost in a stream of consciousness never to be found again, like a dream that you can't quite remember on the tip of your brain, like the feeling you have when you've misplaced something not very important and yet it really irritates you that you don't know where it is. All of this shall pass. While you may not find the words, the meaning is still there, and the search for expression will yield some treasures along the way.

Beautiful Moon

The moon in all her brightness shows her majesty. The moon in all her darkness shows her nuance. The moon in all her stages shows us time. Majesty, nuance, and time do not yet capture her magic. I have spent many nights and even the occasional morning marvelling at the moon's beauty.

Her most vibrant trick is when she is involved in an eclipse, no longer sharing or reflecting light but instead hiding the light from everything or being hidden. How I love the moon in all her incarnations, full and new, crescent and half, and beautiful all the time.

The Bitch About the Beach

I smelled the beach today and regretted that I could not go. The heat was palpable on my skin and in the air for the first time in a long time, that sweet sort of heat that pulls you in and makes you want to be lazy, lying on the sand. The beach was so close, calling to me with that ocean smell, the smell of salt and brine and things hidden just below the surface.

I felt the beach calling me as passersby wearing shorts and sunglasses moved in her direction. The pull for them was strong enough that any fear or danger of gathering seems lost like a distant memory. I felt the beach call me today, but I could not answer, choosing to stay in the safety of the present. Damn if that pandemic isn't a bitch, though.

Not Being Remembered

I remember not being remembered. No one would ask me to sign their yearbook. No one would want to remember. I had the ability to be completely invisible in a crowd.

I remember one girl, one of the popular sort, hearing my voice in a crowded class and wanting to know who was speaking. She could care less when she finally found out the source of the voice.

When I look back, I am grateful for two things: none of these people really mattered, and thank goodness for university. Thank goodness for university.

Six Feet Apart

Masks are not so much about hiding or decoration or expression but for protection. Stay six feet apart.

Temperatures are rising as we are hiding in our masks. Stay six feet apart.

Hiding and biding our time until things get better, stay six feet apart.

How far away should I stay in order to be safe? Stay six feet apart.

How frayed are everyone's nerves in this new normal? Stay six feet apart.

I washed my hands more times than I can count! Stay six feet apart.

I don't want to lose my humanity! Stay six feet apart.

Or the ability to hug the people I love but I know, I know, I should … Stay six feet apart.

The New Blue

You were tempted, weren't you? Tempted by the look and feel of something new. Tempted by a new blue toy to play with. Tempted by more safety features and a much bigger trunk. A rearview camera and all the bells and whistles were just so tempting.

There was nothing wrong with the old. The white toy that you used to play with used to make you happy, don't you remember? But old is old and new is new; white is white and blue is blue. New is nicer and cleaner and so much fun to play with. Enjoy your new toy as much as it will enjoy you.

A Different Path

I stopped today and looked up the street at your place. The construction was still going on with all the trees and shrubs boxed in by wood and orange construction tape. I wanted to walk by and see the construction, see the upheaval and the change. I wanted to be close to the place that had meant so much to me.

I stared for a long time at the construction and the destruction left in the path of all the heavy machinery, and I chose to go in a different direction. Walking past your place would only cause the dog much anxiety when she saw me, the way it always used to. How I miss your place and the dog and, yes, even you. But I am on a different path now, and that does make all the difference.

Gone

Gone. You are gone. The days that we used to remember things by are gone. The view from out the window is gone. The neighbours, both good and bad, are gone. The blue car that we used to zoom around in, gone. The dog who used to love me no matter what is gone. Her carrot ritual is gone. The love we used to share is gone. Gone, but not forgotten. No matter how much time passes and how much distance grows, not forgotten. Not forgotten, but still gone. Long gone. Just gone.

A New Cat

I have a new cat; a new cat I do have, sometimes as sweet as the sunset at night, and sometimes as tumultuous as a red sky in the morning and the storm that follows. He likes to explore his surroundings in silence on four little feet that are padded for quiet. But what's left in his wake shows you where he has been. I have a new cat, a new cat I do have, and I hope my home does survive the experience, along with my nerves.

Without Our Consent

Time passes without our consent. We can choose to fill our time with things that pass the time, like hobbies or work. We can never slow time down or speed time up deliberately. Time may fly while we're having fun, and time may drag while we are waiting for something, but time seems to have a consistency to it. Without our consent, time keeps on slipping into the future. Eventually time will run out, and then perhaps some form of consent will be found, but not so long as time marches on.

The Wild One

The birth of something wild is never an easy thing. You, little one, are definitely something wild. I wonder how it was when you came into the world. Was it kicking and screaming or with the sole purpose of focusing on being wild and out of control? You, little one, are definitely something wild. I watch you move from place to place, disrupting each space that you rush into, leaving nothing unturned in your wake. Everything must be examined and explored, everything climbed in and out of, everything overturned. You, little one, are definitely something wild. Many blessings to you, my little wild one.

The Cat Poem

My cat will not sit still tonight. I secretly think that he wants to write a poem because he keeps trying to take my pen. I wonder what he would write about in the same way that I wonder what he dreams about. Does he need a creative outlet so much that he needs a pen? He's never tried to take paper away, so I think the pen must just be for play.

Sub-poem by Cat

I see a mouse, a mouse I see.
I'll eat that mouse if it goes eek!
When it moves, I'll pounce on it
And thrash it good; it keeps me fit!
I see a mouse, a mouse I see.
Soon it's gone; all's left is me!

Schemes

Seek and Ye shall find.
A few things come to mind.
Water draining in the sink,
The cat rushes in for a drink.
The screen goes black and shuts me out.
I wonder if there's any doubt
That rhyming schemes are hard to do,
Especially smart ones through and through.
The cat returns to play with my pen.
Writing is harder especially when
He bites onto the very end
And the pen can't write poetic bend.

What Follows

Sometimes I think I see something out of the corner of my eye. It will seem like something is moving sometimes. Sometimes it will be very still. Whatever it is, I hope that it isn't actually there. I just know that I don't want whatever it is to be there.

Sometimes I think I sense something behind me, watching, just observing, not wanting to be known, watching and waiting for what happens next. I secretly hope that it means no harm despite its feline stealth.

Sometimes I know something is there. There's nothing I can do at this point. By now, I am dead to rights in its grasp. All that comes next is what follows.

Summertime

Summer seems late this year with the cold and the rain holding on much longer than they normally do. The heat has danced its way in and out of being like a gopher returning to its hole, frightened from seeing its shadow.

How this summer likes to flirt with beaches closing because of E. coli, leaving all of us to wonder and wander away from where we might enjoy the sun in all its glory. Where are we to find pleasure in simple pastimes like getting ice cream or the smell of suntan lotion that signals lazy time out in the sun?

I miss the summer with all its joys, but I do not miss the extreme heat or pollution that can accompany summer. I hope for a balance and a chance to enjoy ice cream anyways.

Missing Out on Home

Sometimes I feel out of place, like I do not have a home. Now don't get me wrong: I have a place to rest my head and to live all the ways a person lives, like making food or doing laundry. But I sometimes have trouble feeling like I can put my heart into the place where I live.

I loved the house I grew up in, with all its old charms and beautiful ways. I loved my grandmother's house with its feeling of old Vancouver, the stucco on the outside and the arches inside. Her beautiful garden was the envy of the neighbourhood.

The place I am now only holds the charms that have carried over from these past places, like the furniture and art, and I am left with a raw feeling in my soul that I am somehow missing out on home.

Beyond the Trees

How I long to know what is beyond the trees, to slip through the vale and be reunited with the ones I love, the ones I miss, the ones I long for. Each day, I look at their pictures on my sacred shelf and miss them. Each day, I wonder if they have encountered one another and turned a tale or two. I wonder if any of these tales are about me, or about what lies beyond the trees. Someday I may know, but for now I will stay here and wonder of tales shared beyond the trees, and of what waits for all of us there.

Devouring Wood

A fire crackles in the fireplace, slowly devouring the wood that has been fed to it. The flames seem like a living thing, dancing and darting and shaking about. This dance of devouring has taken place since the dawn of time. People huddled together for warmth by the fire and stared deeply into the flames, looking for something; they know not what. They were longing for something more than simple warmth from cold bad weather. They were longing for comfort and connection found far, far away, deep inside the wood devoured slowly by the flames of the fire, deep inside the fire that burns unseen, just out of sight, in a place they long for far, far away.

The Leaf

Today, there was a leaf on the kitchen floor. I know because the cat made sure I noticed it. Someone must have dragged it into the house on the bottom of their shoe, only for it to become fodder for the cat. He played with it for a while as I took my breakfast, and, as I finished my meal, poof! The leaf was gone. I don't know where the leaf has gone, but I have a feeling someone knows, and he is not sharing the whereabouts of his new toy with me!

The Inevitable

The things that parents keep from their children—all the hidden things, the unknown things, the embarrassing things, the evil things. If only the world were full of magical rainbows and unicorns, but this is not the case. Change happens, and young curiosity grows. Places and things not yet experienced are sought out, like trying your first cigarette or seeing death for the first time in a way that takes the wind right out of you. Safety and protection are important, but the inevitable is inevitable and we all have so much to lose. Hang on to the unicorns and the rainbows in your memories. Remember the good because the inevitable is inevitable.

Monsters

Masks bring candy once a year. If there is no candy, the monsters appear, egging your house and smashing your pumpkins—a sign that the monsters are displeased.

One year, the monsters came to egg my neighbour's house. I was outside, observing a ritual, when they appeared with all the subtlety of a Mack truck. I put some base in my voice and warned them to leave before the egging began and, suddenly, I was the monster.

At first, they froze, unsure of what to do, so I repeated my warning that it was time to get to stepping and 'poof' they fled into the night. My neighbour's house was spared from a night of mischief. In all the years since, I have never mentioned this night to my neighbours. I prefer to keep my inner monster to myself.

The Grave

Returning to the Earth. It seems all things return to the Earth in the end, ashes to ashes, dust to dust. I've heard it said that we come from the Earth too, but I feel like I need to ponder this imponderable for a while longer for it to be true. All the tiny creatures I see and admire, and love will return to the Earth. It's like the Earth is some great resting place for us to tread upon until we return there. Some giant coffin, waiting to close the lid and swallow us away, to be remembered for as long as a gravestone can communicate its marker. Tread carefully, my friends, and enjoy your time on this great resting place before it's ashes to ashes and dust to dust.

Waking to the Wild One

Wild one, why do you wake me so? I have been asleep for a few hours now, and I see by the clock that it's a little after 4 a.m.! I would still be asleep were it not for your demands to play. Oh, wild one, I do not wake you deliberately when you sleep and expect to be entertained. Surely you can entertain yourself with all the toys you have and all the space you have to run about in. Surely, I do not need to be blinking through bleary eyes into the dark, wondering why I am conscious when I should not be. I love you, wild one, but please let me sleep, baby. My arm can be attacked tomorrow.

Perpetual Darkness

Today has been a day. I feel old and ground down today, as if something has been gnawing on my bones. I feel fatigue flow through me, like thick molasses creeping into the very corners of my being. I do not know how to shake this feeling or the perpetual darkness that seems to sap the light from every part of the day. The shadows do not stir but remain still as the snow collects outside and slowly turns to ice. Today would be a good day to be warmed by a fire but, alas, the shadows call to me, and I must answer, or rest will never come.

Out of Reach

The soul is something intangible and, in many ways, imponderable too. Yet without it we lose our humanity. I sometimes wonder if I damage my soul by focusing on certain things or by not feeding it with healthy things often enough. It seems like my subconscious whispers to me of loss and longing in dreams both waking and at night. Yet when I reach or strive for what is being said, it shrinks back into the shadows with laughter the level of a whisper frustratingly out of reach. I will strive to change the things that are obvious or that make sense, but I often cannot make sense of my subconscious. I guess I will have to keep trying to grasp that which is just out of reach.

New Land

Floating, floating for forty days and forty nights with all those matched animals gathered together. Imagine the smell and the noises, the roars and the squawks. Floating through storms and tempests, like all the struggles of a difficult childbirth for some young mother, imagine all the sleepless nights.

Then the birds went out in search of land and I'm sure what felt like a never-ending passage slowly ended. Imagine the crash to shore and the water slowly ebbing away, leaving this wooden behemoth resting upon a new shore. Was unloading longer than loading? I wonder at the relief they all must have felt arriving in a new land, ready to recreate the Earth.

The Good

I prefer to remember you as living than to think of you as dead. The mail that comes for you now is all returned with 'deceased' on it. People who speak of you speak of you in the past tense. It's amazing to think that one of the things that changed when you passed was the tense that people speak of you in. I miss you, whatever tense you might be, and I regret not having appreciated your sense of humour or your hard work more. Thank you for all that you did for me, for all the early mornings working to secure a better future for me, but most of all thank you for playing catch in the backyard with me. I will hold onto you for as long as I can and try to remember the good.

Admire the Mystery

There are places that exist that you can't go to anymore, ancient places, heritage sites, too old and fragile to be tread upon by human foot. Many of them are so old that they have become a mystery. People think of many reasons why they might exist, but I think an ancient mystery is better. Isn't it better not knowing the truth of certain places on Earth? Isn't it better to admire the mystery that is Stonehenge, or the pyramids (choose any set you please), or Angkor Wat? I like a great mystery, both to ponder and to know that we may never know the complete truth of a place in its prime. Only ancient memories are left now, and the unknown beauty of these places.

The Day the Sirens Came

I

That day, the sirens came, with their wailing and their bee-baw, bee-baw, bee-baw noise. And then the firefighters were there with their many questions, like does she have ID, what medications is she taking, has there been any changes to these medications? All the while I tried to keep up with the mess and the chaos, answering each question as best I could and knowing the many levels of deep exhaustion that lay ahead.

Then the paramedics came, repeating the questions that had been asked by the firefighters, only in more detail. And the mess of it all, with lists of medication and ID getting lost in the shuffle, and sticky-backers from the EKG machine beginning to litter the bed and the floor, and I knew that all of this was the beginning of a deep exhaustion that I might not come back from.

II

Then came the trip from the bedroom down the hall and onto the stairlift. The paramedics had a chair waiting at the bottom of the stairs, a chair which my mother protested there were no arms on for her to use to get into the chair. The wheeling and dealing of rugs and furniture meant more chaos to be tidied later, like some Zen garden trampled by elephants, unaware of the peace that was being disturbed.

Luckily, I remembered to let the cat out of the bathroom, freeing him from his imprisonment, like some criminal falsely accused of nothing. Luckily, I remembered to turn the outside light on, knowing the darkness that will afflict the front of our place, encompassing all like some infection on the soul. And still I knew the deep exhaustion that was to come would start soon.

III

Next came the transfer to the gurney, out on the boulevard with passersby keenly observing my mother wailing like a banshee as she moved onto the gurney. The paramedics asked that I follow in my own vehicle, which of course I don't have, and then grudgingly acquiesced when I asked if I could also travel in the ambulance.

The whole time one of the two paramedics was cracking jokes as I quietly tried to stifle the panic in my belly. The ride to the hospital was bumpy as the shocks in the ambulance were clearly shot, as soon my back would be too. We arrived at the hospital, and I was asked to wait in the waiting room as they began to process my mother into the system. All the while I could feel the exhaustion creeping in at the edges.

IV

The paramedics abandoned us as my mother was transferred to a wheelchair. She then announced that she had to relieve her bladder. I struggled through the door to the bathroom and my back protested as I helped my mother on and off the toilet, and then back out into the waiting room.

My mother then explained that she needed her puffers as she was having trouble breathing. The paramedics had promised us that we could get these puffers at the hospital. I approached the front and asked if my mother could have a puffer. I was told no; we would have to wait to see the doctor for that, which would take at least two hours. I asked what could be done and was told that I should go home in my own vehicle to get the puffers. I gave up, and started to feel strong feelings of exhaustion appear in my psyche as I slowly began to give up on this experience.

V

Two kind things happened next: the arrival of a warm blanket for my mother and the arrival of my best friend, riding in like the cavalry on his bike to lend support.

The blanket was a suggestion from another ER patron who saw my mother in her nightgown and thought she might be cold. She was kind enough to go and get a warm blanket for my mother, like some kind of protection against her fragility. It was a kindness that I was most thankful for.

Next came the arrival of my best friend Geoff. He was a great distraction to me and my mother, both for the horror we were experiencing and the horrors that surrounded us. He chatted and listened and kept our minds off the exhaustion that was now slowly settling into our bones.

VI

After another struggle for my mother to use the bathroom, she expressed again her breathing troubles. At this point I burst into tears. I did not want to lose my composure, but I couldn't handle the situation anymore. The waiting and the horror of it all and my mother being short sent me over the edge, tumbling into tears.

After a moment, Geoff put his arm around me and comforted me as best he could. It was one of many kind things that he did on that visit, and I really needed the support.

After regaining my composure, I approached the front area again and explained about my mother needing a puffer. This time, the nurse explained that there were respiratory nurses that my mother could see who would give her a puffer. I closed my eyes and felt exhausted as I wondered why the nurse two hours earlier did not suggest this. I was also told that the wait for the doctor would be about another two hours.

VII

My mother was wheeled in her wheelchair, covered by a no-longer-warm blanket, to a small area with a chair. The ER nurse tried to get my mother to transfer to the chair, but she refused. The chair was then moved, and my mother was wheeled into the spot where the chair had been. She was given a puff of one of her medications, and shortly after that she was wheeled away for an X-ray.

Geoff had offered to get me some dinner as it was now about two hours past dinnertime and my body was protesting with hunger. I asked him to please bring me whatever he was having. He brought me a falafel, that was wrapped so well that it made it difficult to eat, and a much-needed bottle of water. These helped to stave off the exhaustion I was feeling.

VIII

I bid goodbye to Geoff as my mother returned much worse for wear. She was saying that she was about to throw up, and so the orderly grabbed a vomit bag and a box of tissues and then went on his way. I put my food away, as my mother was then mildly ill. After helping her to clean up, she began screaming from a pain in her side. She just kept screaming "Oh, the pain" louder and louder. The thing that amazed me was how other than the orderly, no one did anything to help her. I did my best to comfort her by holding her hand. She continued to wail, "the pain." As time passed and everyone ignored us, eventually someone came and said a bed had become open in the triage area and my mother was being transferred there. I followed along behind her as she was wheeled to the bed, all the while feeling true exhaustion seep in.

IX

As my mother climbed into the bed, I noticed there was no pillow. I went back to the desk where we had just been and asked for a pillow. I was told that there were no pillows, but I could have a couple of blankets instead to make a pillow out of. I took the blankets and returned to my mother, making her as comfortable as I could with these makeshift pillows. She passed right out.

She slept in a truly exhausted way for about an hour and a half. When she woke up, she asked me where the TV clicker was. She said she wanted to turn off the view from her bed as it was bothering her. I laughed, and then I asked her if she knew where she was. Eventually it all came flooding back. I hated to see her realize where she was and what was happening. Soon after, she began pleading to go home as the time slowly crept past eleven at night.

X

Then the doctor came, asking questions that my mother was deliberately obtuse about. When asked why she was there, she told the doctor that I had made her call 9-1-1, blaming me for all that had happened. The doctor repeated some bloodwork and an EKG and came back an hour later saying that my mother's heart was fine, and we could go.

I explained that she was also experiencing severe gut pains, and the doctor said that he would have one more test done. My mother complained that she just wanted to go home. All the while, true exhaustion began encompassing me to my core.

XI

My mother went for her final test this visit with me tagging along behind her as she went. We arrived at a waiting bay, and my mother was left in a spot to eventually be wheeled into the exam room. She began to complain of having breathing issues again. Shortly thereafter, one of the lab technicians discovered my mother's puffer from earlier in the evening on the back of a wheelchair. My mother asked for the puffer, but I said I didn't think it was a good idea.

My mother then went for a scan, and I could hear her struggling and screaming on the other side of the door, and all I could think was, "What is happening?" And I let myself feel the exhaustion come, almost like an old friend now, welcoming me to I know not what.

XII

When we returned to the bed spot, I went and told the doctor about my mother needing another puffer. One came shortly thereafter. The doctor then returned and said that my mother had lesions on her liver and that he recommended an outpatient MRI to define these lesions. He emphasized 'outpatient' a little too strongly. My mother also got a prescription for an antacid that ended up later doing her no good. With that, we were released.

I called for a taxi as soon as we got outside. They said it would be at least half an hour. My mother was rightfully upset, and so we waited in the cool of the night for a taxi to come and return us to our upturned home.

Hello, exhaustion.

For Geoff

How I love to see you, my friend. Our time together is rarer now and more difficult to find. I enjoy our time together and the conversations that follow.

I miss who we were in our younger days, seeking ourselves in new and interesting ways. I miss sharing who we were becoming in our twenties and supporting each other along the way. I am proud and blessed to know the man you have become.

Our friendship has seen many phases, good and bad, beautiful and ugly, yet I have always felt that you have had my back. Thank you for your love and support all these years. We have changed, but our friendship has remained close.

I Left My Brain in My Other Coat Pocket

One time, I left my brain in my other coat pocket.
I was without my poor brain for quite some time.
Thinking was hard and intellectualizing even harder.
Never try to intellectualize without your brain.
Nasty bit of business, that.
One time, I left my brain in my other coat pocket.
Now if only I knew where my pancreas was.

Little Bird

Little bird, thank you for coming and sharing yourself with me each day. Your voice is so beautiful, and watching you hop and flutter about outside my kitchen window brings me such joy. You seem so intently interested in coming inside to visit me. I somehow wonder if you carry the spirit of someone who belonged here from the past with you, and if that spirit has carried you back here to find me. Thank you for your beauty and your spirit and for coming to see me each morning as I have my breakfast.

Yuki the cat thanks you too.

Precipice

Last gasp. I hold your hand. Someone murmurs a prayer. How many times does one come to the precipice before falling over? No more live streaming, just real life. I'm still not sure what you mean by that. Maybe someday everything will make sense, but today, precipice …

The Vale

You told me about the vale once, and how you wanted to slip through it. Everyone you've ever known who is no longer here is there on the other side. You wanted to wait until the vale was at its thinnest and then slip through, like a key in a keyhole. Your father would be waiting, waiting there for you. You were always meant to be together, and now you can be.

Now, you are on the other side of the vale, and I yearn to see you again. Perhaps I'll wait until the vale is nice and thin to visit you. Or I may just wait until I am on the other side of the vale. I'll look for you there. I'll find you again.

The Mouse

Today, my cat found another mouse. Today, I am going to have to quietly slip on my shoes while my cat 'plays' with this newfound mouse. Ominously, the closet door opens and closes as I slide into my sandals.

The cat continues to bat the mouse around the floor, and when the mouse tries to make a break for it, the cat picks the mouse up in his mouth and brings it back to where he wants it.

I kick the poor thing off the rug and out onto the hardwood floor. I raise up with my right foot and, a moment later, only two hearts beat where once there were three.

I tend to cleaning up the mess left behind, feeling guilty for what I have done but knowing that what happened had to happen.

Birthdays

The land shifts and changes again from sun to dark, season to season. Somewhere amid all of this change another birthday comes, announcing another number to change as well, another candle to contend with.

How many birthdays is it again now? How many candles count the years gone by? If I said your age, would you regret others hearing the number?

Let your age come unto you just as the seasons do, each in their turn. Enjoy the little differences and end those fiery candles with a might blow! Happy Birthday.

Back to Bed

Breakfast's burning, sleep is yearning, the day cannot start again.

Tail's afire, fleeing's the desire, let's try this one over, my friend.

Coffee's brewing, house a ruin, I am covered in cat hair.

Where's the lint roller for all this shed? Where's my toque to warm my head? I am going back to bed.

The Snow

When I was a child, my mother did not like the snow. Whenever it snowed, my mother would look out the window and say, "Oh shit!" She would hit the s-word particularly hard each time.

One time, my godmother Ollie, who was also my mother's best friend, was visiting us. It began to snow very gently and sweetly outside. I took Ollie by the hand and led her to the window. I pointed outside to the gently falling snow and said, "Look Ollie, oh shit!"

Despite my godmother's horror, my mother continued to curse the snow until she finally moved away from snow-bearing climates.

Dark Days

Dark days are here again. Cold, wet, snowy, dark, damp, lightless dreary days are here again. My mood always flickers like a candle on a windowsill at this time of year. I yearn for the light and wish I could escape this space and place for somewhere brighter.

Somewhere where the pitter patter of the rain doesn't keep you up at night. Someplace where you don't find yourself thinking, "The sky has gotten dark again." Someplace where the light stops that candle from flickering. Someplace … warm.

The Cork

A cork. A single cork. Nothing holds my cat's attention as much as this single cork. I had the idea while at a gathering on New Year's Eve. When the bottle went pop, I asked the host to save the cork for me.

Upon returning home, the first thing I did was throw the cork up in the air to my cat, and he hasn't stopped playing with it since. As the cork bobs and spins and spirals all around, my cat keenly follows and actively hunts the cork. He even carries it around in his mouth as I have seen him do with mice: a prized possession to be kept close and played with.

Afraid

Sometimes I'm afraid of things that make no sense, like goblins and gremlins and things just out of sight under beds and in closets and on the top of bookcases.

Sometimes I'm afraid of things that do make sense, like taxes and bills and cleaning the gunk out of the bottom of the sink after doing the dishes.

Sometimes real things scare me, like death and loss and pain and being alone. I will say this, though: I'm getting kind of tired of being afraid. Or, perhaps put differently, I'm tired of there being so many things to be afraid of.

Crow

Hello, crow. I cannot help but recognize that you are staring that sideways glance of yours at me. Do you have a question for me, buried in those deep black eyes that seem to go on forever? Or are you looking for more than conversation as you stare at me, dark orbs unmoving?

I feel I have no answers for you today, only a fond hello and a keen admiration for one as clever as you. I hope your dark eyes and equally dark wings lead you to many good places. I wish you well, little crow. Now, see if the next one is more interesting than me.

Dreams

I have so many dreams that are fleeting in the night. Fleeting like the night, they come and go, sometimes chasing me through frightening landscapes, sometimes reminding me of days and people gone by.

I feel like dreams creep as if slowly crawling through a land of jagged edges and many steps up and down, so many steps that M. C. Escher would be proud: a Salvador Dali painting come to life.

Dreams, these seamless things, let me rest inside a dream for one more night.

Chopsticks

Chopsticks. Magical chopsticks. Somehow, the chopsticks I left by the side of the sink to be washed have wound up on the floor by my bed. As I awoke and went to put my slippers on, there they were, magical chopsticks on the floor.

As I arose and went downstairs, magical chopsticks in hand, the cat greeted me. The look on his face was as if to say, "Oh, you found those things I hunted up for you. Good!" He seemed so proud.

I put the chopsticks back by the sink only to hear that cat playing with them again shortly thereafter. Somehow, the magic went out of the chopsticks as they wound up the proud possession of my cat once again.